New Start Suspense Series

Part 2

Resource Guide

By

Patricia Birtwistle

Copyright 2015 by Patricia J. Birtwistle
All Rights Reserved

ISBN 978-0-9947326-2-0

No part of this publication may be reproduced, stored in or introduced into a retrieval system, or transmitted, in any form, or by any means (electronic, mechanical, photocopying, recording or otherwise) without the prior written permission of both the copyright owner and the publisher of this book.

Patnor Publishing

ACKNOWLEDGMENTS

Once again my heartfelt thanks to Pat Nelson. She has been my helpmate and friend throughout this process. Thanks also to Sharon Kirk and Mary Ann Phelps for their editing, Linda Ciocci for previewing and Taralynn Disher for her cover illustrations.

New Start Suspense Series

Part 2

Resource Guide

Table of Contents

		Page
About the Author		5
New Start Suspense Series - Part 2 Rationale		6
The Hermit	Chapter Synopsis	7-8
	Student Worksheets Chapters 1-8	9-25
	Student Worksheets Answer Key	26-30
	Skills List Teacher's Guide	31
	Skills List Student Evaluation	32
	New Vocabulary List by Chapter	33
	New Vocabulary List	34
My Secret	Chapter Synopsis	35-36
	Student Worksheets Chapters 1-8	37-52
	Student Worksheets Answer Key	53-57
	Skills List Teacher's Guide	58
	Skills List Student Evaluation	59
	New Vocabulary List by Chapter	60
	New Vocabulary List	61

About the Author

Patricia Birtwistle was a teacher and consultant of Special Education for most of her career. One of her biggest challenges was finding appropriate reading materials for the many and varied student learning needs within the boundaries of her jurisdiction.

After being retired for a number of years, Patricia was asked to find some reading materials for a sixteen-year-old brain injured young man. She searched libraries, bookstores and catalogues to no avail. It was then that Patricia began writing this series and she looks forward to seeing them in the hands of many young people who need or want to read.

Objectives

To fill the gap in the literary field by providing high interest, low vocabulary novelettes for reluctant readers, English as a Second Language students, the brain injured and the learning disabled.

Education

Principal Certificate

Specialist in Special Education

B.A. – University of Western Ontario

Experience

Student Services Consultant – Welland County Separate School Board

Programming assistance for Teachers: Team Leader of Student Services Group consisting of a Psychologist, Speech Pathologist, Teacher for the Gifted, Resource Teacher and Diagnostician

Assisted Teachers/Parents in locating materials for Special Education students in the segregated classes

Assessed needs of students

Programming assistance for Teachers

Liaison Teacher for Special Education – Welland County Separate School Board

Special Education Teacher – Welland County Separate School Board

Taught grades 7 and 8 Middlesex County Roman Catholic School Board

Principal Middlesex County Roman Catholic School Board

Elementary Teacher Middlesex County Roman Catholic School Board

New Start Suspense Series – PART 2 RATIONALE

The main objective in the **New Start Suspense Series – Part 2** is to close the gap between the controlled and basic vocabulary in Part 1 (set at a grade 2-3 reading level) and the regular reading level of grades 3-4. The vocabulary found in Part 1 of the Series ensured that readers were comfortable while maintaining interest. This comfort level was the primary goal of Part 1.

The first series of books was written for students in grades 4 and up who have a very limited reading vocabulary. The objective was to gradually build on that vocabulary while maintaining interest and developing reading skills. The author believes that once students have completed Part 1 of the Series they are confident enough to move to more challenging material. This transition should be gradual in order that readers not get discouraged and lose the comfort gained with reading. It is for this reason that Part 2 has been written. The skills and vocabulary are still somewhat controlled but not to the extent that they were in Part 1. By the time students have completed Part 2 it is hoped that they will be able to read more difficult material at the grade four level with comfort.

New Start Suspense Series Part 2 revolves around the same young people who were introduced in Part 1. However, in Part 2 the vocabulary is expanded much more quickly. There are more chapters and chapters are longer. Pictures are not included as discussed in Part 1 for two reasons: students learn to read pictures rather than developing reading skills and the novelettes endeavor to appear as much as possible as any other novel.

Worksheets included (**ALL WORKSHEETS MAY BE COPIED**) are more difficult both in content and writing skills. They cover skills for the instructor's assessment in the following areas:

- Word Study
- Character Study
- Main Idea
- Inference
- Sequence
- Cause and Effect
- Reading for Detail
- Using Context Clues
- Predicting Outcome
- Critical Thinking

THE HERMIT

Chapter Synopsis

CHAPTER 1

The group had picked out a perfect spot for a camping week-end. They rush to get set up and begin exploring. As they settle down for the night, someone comes to the camp. Nick is startled awake by the prowler. He is reluctant to wake up the others.

CHAPTER 2

In exploring the rock hills, the kids see someone down by the lake. Dan and Bob decide to climb down the cliff. On the descent, Dan injures his hand. Bob leaves him to get down to the lake to ask the man for help. Rather than helping, the man chases Bob.

CHAPTER 3

Nick, Beth and Kim know that they will have to help Dan out of his mess. Nick gets rope and tries to get one of the girls to take one end down to Dan. Failing that, they lower one end down to Dan. Dan then ties himself off and the three kids begin pulling him up the cliff. All goes well until Nick sees a thin spot in the rope and is afraid if they go any further the rope will snap.

CHAPTER 4

It is a long difficult task trying to get Dan up the cliff. A rock comes loose and almost hits Dan. He is loosing feeling in his good hand and is feeling faint. To add to their problems, Nick thinks he has seen someone watching them. They finally succeed getting Dan up over the edge but by then he has fainted.

CHAPTER 5

As Bob returns to the campsite he mulls over the encounter with the hermit. When he reaches the camp, he realizes that someone has been there and upset their things. He is disturbed that the others have not returned so he lights a campfire hoping they will smell the smoke and return to camp.

CHAPTER 6

Surprisingly Dan comes to and doesn't seem too badly hurt. The four kids return to camp. They decide to explore the bush. When that proves uninteresting they go fishing. When they return to their camp at dusk, they find the campsite a mess with things strewn all over.

CHAPTER 7

The kids debate returning home but decide against it because it is too late in the day. They also decide to make the most of their last night out. They exchange stories about their parents. After the girls retire, Bob tells Nick and Dan about his encounter with the hermit.

CHAPTER 8

Bob is awakened at dawn thinking someone is moving around the camp. Someone or something hits the girls' tent. All of this is enough to make the group pack up and head home early. When they report what happened on the week-end, they expect their parents to take some action against the hermit. However, the parents know from past history that the hermit is harmless. They finally admit that they (the parents) were the ones who had been disrupting things at the camp all week-end.

The Hermit

Chapter 1

Name _____

Cause and Effect   Find or write the answer

1. The girls' tent "was up in a flash" because

   _____.

2. "It didn't take them long to make a fire pit." That was because

   _____.

3. Why could the kids see the cobwebs so well? It was because of the

   _____.

4. What made the boys get upset with the girls on the path? The girls let

   on they were _____.

5. What made Nick sit up in his tent?

   _____.

Main Idea

   What is this chapter about?

   _____.

Details

1. It let out a cry and hit out at Bob _____.

2. They had lots of food because they had made a _____.

3. They left the food in their _____.

4. The boys said that there were bears in the woods because there were

   _____.

5. Nick did not yell when he saw _____.

Inference

      afraid   food   bush   others

1. Nick did not yell because he would upset the _____.

2. The raccoon hit out at Bob because it was _____.

3. Nick said "I could eat a horse" because he wanted _____.

4. They thought they would have trouble because of _____.

5. The spot was a good one to explore because of the _____.

Critical Thinking

Do you think that Nick should yell to the others? Yes or No? Why or why not?

_____

_____.

The Hermit

Chapter 2

Name _____

Word Study   **Match**

_____   headed out   a)   did not go

_____   quiet   b)   bled

_____   held their ground   c)   move about softly

_____   shed his blood   d)   began to go

_____   waving   e)   moving back and forth

Character Study

1. Who seems to be the most fun? Why?

   _____

   _____

2. Who do you think acts the oldest? Why?

   _____

   _____

3. Which girl do you like best? Why?

   _____

   _____

Details   Yes or No

1. They said they would come back at noon to keep Beth happy. _____

2. The man seemed to be looking for something in the water. _____

3. The man looked up when Dan yelled. _____

4. The man got mad as soon as he saw Bob. _____

Context Clues

1. Nick was good at thinking ahead because he _____

2. Kim was good at thinking ahead, too. She could see that they could not _____.

3. Dan didn't believe Nick had seen someone outside the tent because he _____.

4. Bob could help hold Dan up so he must be _____

5. Nick is good at planning. The story tells us this because _____.

6. What do you think Dan will do? _____.

The Hermit

Chapter 3

Name_____

Context Clues

1. Who do you think is in the biggest trouble? _____.

   Why? _____.

Inference

2. It must have been hot out. We think that because

   _____.

Character Study

3. In this chapter we find that Dan is _____.

   We know that because he _____.

Sequence   Number the statements in order

4. _____   The girls would not go down the hill.

5. _____   Nick got some rope from the camp.

6. _____   Nick saw a thin spot on the rope.

7. _____   The rope got stuck on the rocks.

8. _____   They took a rest.

9. _____   Dan came off the ground on the rope.

Critical Thinking

10.   Do you think that the girls should have gone down to help Dan? Why or why not?

_____

_____

_____

The Hermit

Chapter 4

Name _____

Word Study　　　　Fill in the blanks with these words

knew　　　　know　　　　edge　　　　their　　　　ground　　　　no

new　　　　there

1. The _____ was soft.

2. Beth was on _____.

3. The girls had rope in _____ tent.

4. The rope went over the _____ of the rocks.

5. They _____ what to do.

6. They held their _____.

7. The campsite was _____ to the kids.

8. They didn't _____ what to do.

Cause and Effect　　　Find the answer in the chapter

9. The rock fell because of _____.

10. Getting Dan up took a long time and this made him
   _____.

11. The rope could split because of the _____ spot.

12. Nick, Beth and Kim went into the bush because Nick had
   _____.

13. Dan was sobbing because he _____.

Main Idea

14. What is this chapter about?
   _____

Details   Yes or No

15. Bob helped Nick at the edge of the rocks. _____

16. The kids felt someone was in the bush. _____

17. Dan did his best to help. _____

18. A rock fell and hit Dan. _____

19. Kim knew Dan was okay because he looked up at her. _____

Predicting Outcomes

20. What do you think will happen next?
   _____
   _____.

21. Why do you think that?

   _____

   _____.

The Hermit
Chapter 5

Name _____

Character Study

1. The Hermit was thinking that he should "just get out of here." That makes us think that _____.

Context Clues

2. The Hermit was not at the camp this time when the kids were not there. How do we know that?

   _____.

Inference   Check all the things we know from this chapter

3. _____ The hermit did not want trouble.

   _____ Bob wanted to get back and help out with Dan.

   _____ The kids had all come back to camp.

   _____ At first Bob had forgotten about the hermit.

   _____ Bob was not afraid when the Hermit came at him.

   _____ The man by the water was the Hermit.

   _____ Bob did not think that anyone had been at the camp.

   _____ Bob didn't like being by himself.

   _____ Bob wanted to go back and help with Dan.

   _____ Getting a fire going would help get the others back to camp.

Cause and Effect   Write in a complete sentence

4. Bob could make the camping trip end. How could he do that?

_____

_____.

Critical Thinking

5. What trouble is Dan having?

_____

_____.

6. What trouble is Bob having?

_____

_____.

7. Which one is in the biggest trouble and why do you think that?

_____

_____.

The Hermit

Chapter 6

Name _____

Word Study   Choose the best word from this list

   cut away   quiet   died   on edge   woods

1. their laughing stopped _____
2. the hill kept going down fast _____
3. the kids were jumpy _____
4. they went into the bush _____
5. they kept still _____

Sequence Number these as they happened in the chapter

1. _____ They were laughing as they got back to camp.
2. _____ Dusk came before they knew it.
3. _____ After they ate they put the rest of the food away.
4. _____ Dan went to the tent to put something on his hand.
5. _____ They picked up wood for the fire.
6. _____ His one leg began kicking just a little.

Detail   Who?

1. _____ thought that the fire Bob made was too big.

2. _____ thought they should eat something.

3. _____ did not tell them about the Hermit.

4. _____ wanted to go fishing.

5. _____ had never fished before.

Inference

1. The kids knew Dan would be okay. Why?
   _____

2. Dan wanted to go back to camp by himself. Why?
   _____

3. The kids thought that Dan must have hit his head. Why?
   _____

4. Bob didn't want to go back to the lake to fish. Why?
   _____

5. The kids were quiet when they were fishing. Why?
   _____

Predicting Outcomes

What do you think will happen to the kids the last night of camping?

_____

_____

The Hermit

Chapter 7

Name _____

Main Idea

1. What is this chapter about?
   _____

Inference What do the words in **bold print** mean?

2. Kim said someone came to "**mess with our stuff**"
   _____

3. Nick said they should "**stick it out**".
   _____

4. Beth said they were "**trapped here**".
   _____

5. The story talks about "**the spot they were in**".
   _____

6. Bob said the person was "**not out to get us**".
   _____

Character Study From this chapter tell 2 things you know about

Dan 1) _____

Why do you think that? _____

2) _____

What makes you think that? _____

Cause and Effect   **Match**

The kids were not at home so they	the kids were laughing
Dan told funny stories so	could not stay up
It was dark so that made the kids	could tell stories about their folks
Telling stories	made time go faster
The boys had a bad day so they	stay at the camp

Critical Thinking

The kids stayed at the camp for the night. What do you think they should have done? Why?

_____

_____

The Hermit

Chapter 8

Name _____

Main Idea

1. What would be a good name for this chapter?
   _____

Sequence   Number the things as they happened

2. _____ They packed to go home.

3. _____ They told their folks about their trouble when they got home.

4. _____ Bob saw tracks by the bush.

5. _____ Their folks had a good laugh.

6. _____ Someone hit the girls' tent.

7. _____ They all went to Beth's house.

Details

1. Why did Bob sit up? _____

2. What did Bob find at the edge of the bush? _____

3. What did they put on the fire to put it out? _____

4. What surprised the kids when they told their folks about the

   trouble? _____

Context Clues   Answer in a full sentence.

1. The kids must like Dan. How do you know that from this chapter?
   _____

2. It had been a bad day. What happened that makes us believe this?
   _____

3. The folks had all planned to go to Beth's house. How do we know that? _____

4. There would not be trouble for the Hermit. Why?
   _____

Predicting Outcomes

What do you think the kids will do once they find out what their folks did?

_____

THE HERMIT

ANSWER KEY – Students WORKSHEETS

Chapters 1-8

CHAPTER 1

Cause and Effect

1. they practiced
2. there was lots of wood around the camp.
3. sunlight
4. eating something
5. something or someone was moving outside

Main Idea

Setting up camp.

Details

1. raccoon
2. list
3. backpacks
4. raccoons
5. something moving

Inference

1. others
2. afraid
3. food
4. Dan
5. bush

Critical Thinking

Answers will vary

CHAPTER 2

Word Study

d, c, a, b, e,

Character Study

Answers will vary

Detail

1. no
2. yes
3. no
4. yes

Context Clues

1. brought rope
2. help Dan with some rope
3. wanted to come back to camp at noon
4. strong
5. answers will vary
6. answers will vary

CHAPTER 3

Context Clues

1. answers will vary

Inference

2. Various statements that the kids were dripping wet after exertion.

Character Study

3. Answers will vary. Dan kept yelling

Sequence

4. 2
5. 1
6. 6
7. 3
8. 5
9. 4

Critical Thinking

10. Answers will vary.

CHAPTER 4

Word Study

1. ground
2. edge
3. their
4. edge

5. knew
6. ground
7. new
8. know

Cause and Effect

9. the rope
10. pass out
11. thin
12. seen something
13. hurt

Main Idea

14. This chapter is about getting Dan up the hill. (Answers may vary somewhat.)

Details

15. No
16. Yes
17. Yes
18. No
19. No

Predicting Outcomes

20. Answers will vary.
21. Answers will vary.

CHAPTER 5

Character Study

1. He did not want any trouble. Answers will vary.

Context Clues

2. The hermit was chasing Bob.

Inference

3. –   The Hermit did not want trouble.
    - At first Bob had forgotten about the hermit.
    - The man by the water was the Hermit.
    - Bob didn't like being by himself.
    - Getting a fire going would help get the others back to camp.

Cause and Effect

4. He could tell them about the Hermit.

Critical Thinking

5. Dan is stuck on the rocks.
6. Bob has trouble with the Hermit
7. Answers will vary.

CHAPTER 6

Word Study

1. died
2. cut away
3. on edge
4. woods
5. quiet

Sequence

6, 5, 4, 3, 2, 1,

Detail

1. Nick
2. Kim
3. Bob
4. Dan
5. Beth

Inference

1. His colour was coming back (or) he got up (or) he began talking
2. He felt badly for ruining their afternoon (variation of)
3. He was acting normal (or crazy) after what had happened
4. He was afraid the Hermit would be there
5. They were remembering the trouble they had all day

Predicting Outcomes

Answers will vary.

CHAPTER 7

Main Idea

1. Answers will vary.

Inference

2. Go through or move
3. Stay
4. Can't leave

5. Trouble they are in
6. Won't hurt us

Character Study

Answers will vary.

Cause and Effect

- could tell stories about their folks
- the kids were laughing
- stay at the camp
- made time go fast
- could not stay up

Critical Thinking

Answers will vary.

CHAPTER 8

Main Idea

1. answers will vary

Sequence

2. 3
3. 4
4. 2
5. 6
6. 1
7. 5

Details

1. heard something
2. tracks
3. mud
4. their folks didn't seem upset

Context Clues

1. They didn't tell their folks about Dan getting into trouble.
2. They went to sleep in no time.
3. They all got there at the same time.
4. He didn't do anything.

Predicting Outcomes

Answers will vary.

The Hermit

Skills List

	Chapter 1	Chapter 2	Chapter 3	Chapter 4	Chapter 5	Chapter 6	Chapter 7	Chapter 8
Word Study		✓		✓		✓		
Character		✓	✓		✓		✓	
Main Idea	✓			✓			✓	✓
Inference	✓		✓		✓	✓	✓	
Sequence	✓		✓			✓		✓
Cause/Effect	✓			✓	✓		✓	
Detail		✓		✓		✓		✓
Context Clues		✓	✓		✓			✓
Predicting Outcomes		✓		✓		✓		✓
Critical Thinking	✓		✓		✓		✓	

The Hermit

Skills List

Student's Name _____

	Chapter 1	Chapter 2	Chapter 3	Chapter 4	Chapter 5	Chapter 6	Chapter 7	Chapter 8
Word Study								
Character								
Main Idea								
Inference								
Sequence								
Cause/ Effect								
Detail								
Context Clues								
Predicting Outcomes								
Critical Thinking								

The Hermit

List of New Vocabulary by Chapter

Chapter 1	Chapter 2	Chapter 3	Chapter 4
- anyone - beautiful - camping - dark - edge - ever - explore - forgot - forward - hope - knew - laugh - light - others - pull - rope - story	- ate - check - food - ground - hear - held - shed - tent - quiet	- afraid - around - feet - move - split - thin	- been - but - crazy - long - something - their - thought

Chapter 5	Chapter 6	Chapter 7	Chapter 8
- fishing - part - remembered - sometime - surprise - watching - wood	- acting - ate - eat - give - heard - never - once	- about - great - long - right	- believe - happened - talked

The Hermit – New Vocabulary List

A
- about
- acting
- afraid
- anyone
- around
- ate

B
- beautiful
- been
- believe
- but

C
- camping
- check
- crazy

D
- dark

E
- eat
- edge
- ever
- explore

F
- feet
- fishing
- five
- food
- forgot
- forward

G
- give
- great
- ground

H
- happened
- hear
- heard
- held
- hope

K
- knew

L
- laugh
- light
- long

M
- move

N
- never

O
- once
- others

P
- pull

Q
- quiet

R
- remembered
- right
- rope

S
- shed
- something
- sometime
- split
- surprise
- story

T
- talked
- tent
- their
- thin
- thought

W
- watching
- wood

My Secret

Chapter Synopsis

CHAPTER 1

Tom is unpacking his belongings in his new home. He is distraught because he is in his last year and must start at a new school. He thinks of all the troubles he has faced over the years and doesn't know if he'll be able to finish his schooling. He wonders what he should do and is so upset he lies down.

CHAPTER 2

Tom sets out for school still unsure of whether he will go in or not. He forces himself and gets through the day without too much trouble. On the way home Dan catches up with him and offers his friendship. When Tom finally is in his room, he begins planning his survival moves that will help him make it to the end of the school year.

CHAPTER 3

The bullies have watched Tom and just began to terrorize him when he joined the school's ball team. This lifts his spirits and he begins to enjoy school. That's when one teacher begins giving him a hard time. This has happened to Tom before and he is fearful of what might happen.

CHAPTER 4

The group goes out for something to eat and spend their time talking about the new kid. They are worried that if they befriend him it might make trouble for them. They feel sorry for him but the group is split on whether to help him or not. Nick decides to take on the task of trying to figure out who Tom is.

CHAPTER 5

Nick begins observing Tom more closely. In doing so he becomes more aware of the bullies' actions. Nick gets so angry, he asks the kids to get together to discuss what is happening. Although the others know about the bullying they don't seem to want to get involved. They want to focus on Tom.

CHAPTER 6

Nick admits he can't figure out what's wrong with Tom. They don't think that even though Mr. Black picks on Tom that it is the problem. Because the rest of the group has been watching, they are more acutely aware of the extent of the bullying. They decide to each befriend one kid who is being bullied. They will also try to figure out what is bugging Tom.

CHAPTER 7

Dan catches up to Tom on their way home from school. Tom changes the subject when Dan tries to question him. After the game the next day, the team met to plan a fund raiser – powderpuff football. Beth asks Tom if she can "fill in" as his girlfriend for the game. After the successful game, the team celebrates. When everyone leaves except the group of five and Tom, they question him about bullying.

CHAPTER 8

The kids start a "stand beside" plan in order to stop the bullies. Tom tells Beth his secret and she does what she can to help him. The "stand beside" program takes off. Many of the kids in the school pick up on it and begin practicing it on their own. The bullies begin to back down. Tom graduates and can move on with his dream. He never tells us his secret.

My Secret

Chapter 1

Name_____

Character Study

1. The mom is kind because she
   _____

2. We know the kid does not give up. How do we know that?
   _____

Inference

3. He must be a good kid that others like. We know this because
   _____

Cause and Effect   Find the answer in this chapter.

4. He did not like school so he _____

5. His folks wanted him to be happy so they
   _____

6. He lay down because _____

7. He didn't tell his folks his secret. Why?
   _____

8. Things worked out in his old school. Why?
   _____

Sequence Number each item as it happened in this chapter.

9. _____ he packed his things

10. _____ he went to bed

11. _____ his dad got a new job

12. _____ he begged his folks to let him stay

13. _____ he played sick

14. _____ he is making plans

Critical Thinking

15. What do you think he is planning?

   _____

16. Why do you think that?

   _____

My Secret

Chapter 2

Name_____

Word Study   Fill in the blanks with these words.

dream   cute   shower   friend   problem   toward

1. Someone you like. _____

2. Something you want _____

3. To move to _____

4. A fall of water _____

5. Something hard _____

6. Good to look at _____

Main Idea

What is chapter 2 about?

_____

Inference

We know Tom is:

- afraid because _____
- kind because _____
- a loner because _____

Context Clues

1. Tom is always making plans. This makes us think that
   _____

2. He doesn't want to make friends because
   _____

3. Kids must like him because
   _____

Predicting Outcome

What do you think will happen to Tom?
_____

My Secret

Chapter 3

Name _____

Word Study   Underline a word meaning.

1. **not the same** – Kids who are a little different and have no friends.

2. **some kids who are not kind** – It didn't take the bullies long to find Tom.

3. **a school class** – I was in history with Mr. Black.

4. **one with others** – I was part of the school's team.

5. **needing more** – We are a man short for the team.

Details

1. What two things did Tom do with his time before he was on the team?
   _____

2. Tom had two things in mind that made him want to be on the team. What were they?
   _____

Cause and Effect

Why was Mr. Black picking on Tom?

1. _____

2. _____

Context Clues

"I seem to take one step forward and two steps back." When Tom says that he is telling us that

_____

Critical Thinking

Tom is trying to get Mr. Black to stop picking on him. He tried some things. What is something else you would do if you were Tom?

_____

_____

My Secret

Chapter 4

Name _____

Main Idea

What is this chapter about?

_____

Sequence   List these in the order they happened.

- Bob left
- Beth's face got red
- Nick and Dan stopped to talk
- Beth left
- Tom went by
- Nick said to give it some time

1. _____
2. _____
3. _____
4. _____
5. _____
6. _____

Details   one answer for each

1. Who wants to make friend's with Tom and why?
   _____

2. Who is afraid to make friend's with Tom and why?
   _____

Character Study

1. What is one thing Tom did that makes the kids

   - think that he is trouble _____

   - think he is a good kid _____

Critical Thinking

Would you make friends with Tom? Why or why not?

_____

_____

My Secret

Chapter 5

Name _____

Details

What are two things the bullies did to Tom?

1. _____
2. _____

Inference

When Nick told the others about the bullies they "were not surprised".

Why? _____

Character Study

The chapter tells us that Tom was "hard to read". Name two things he does that make him "hard to read".

1. _____
2. _____

Context Clues

Tom has met bullies before. We know this because

_____

Predicting Outcome

Do you think the kids will do something about the bullies? Yes or No.

Name 2 things you think they will do if you said "Yes".

    1. _____

    2. _____

Name 2 things why you think they will not do anything.

    1. _____

    2. _____

My Secret

Chapter 6

Name _____

Word Study   Write the new words beside what they mean.

each   great   mine   week   mean

1. belongs to me _____

2. everyone _____

3. likable _____

4. not kind _____

5. seven days _____

Main Idea

What is this chapter about?

_____

Sequence   Number these how they happened.

_____   Kim spoke up.

_____   Bob said the problem was too big for them.

_____   Nick felt lost about helping Tom.

_____   Each kid picks someone to help.

_____   Dan says he'll try to help Tom.

_____   Bob went online.

Cause and Effect

Nick doesn't get angry. Why is he angry now?

_____

Critical Thinking

What are two things you think the kids could do to stop the bullies.

1. _____

2. _____

My Secret

Chapter 7

Name _____

Word Study   Some words have more than one meaning. Tell the meaning of the word with a line under it.

1. others think they are <u>cool</u>

   _____

2. had a <u>great</u> time

   _____

3. we had to <u>part</u> ways

   _____

4. it wouldn't take them <u>long</u>

   _____

Cause and Effect

Tom had friends who found out his secret. Two things happened when they helped him. What were they?

1. _____

2. _____

Detail

When Tom thought Dan was going to ask him something about himself he stopped him. How did he do this?

_____

Context Clues

What surprised Tom in this chapter? Why did this surprise him?

_____

_____

Predicting Outcome

What do you think will happen to Tom in the last chapter? What makes you think that?

_____

My Secret

Chapter 8

Name _____

Character Study

Tom talks about himself during this novel. Write three things you know about him and tell how you know this.

1. _____
   _____

2. _____
   _____

3. _____
   _____

Main Idea

If you were to give a title to this chapter, what would you name it?

_____

Inference

We know that the group of five would make great friends to have. We know that because _____

Predicting Outcome

Write a different ending to this chapter.

_____

_____

_____

Critical Thinking

Why do you think we are not told the secret?

_____

_____

_____

My Secret

Student WORKSHEETS Answer Key

CHAPTER 1

Character Study

1. took time to sit with him or tried to make him feel better
2. he kept going back to school

Inference

3. He had friends.

Cause and Effect

4. played sick
5. bought (got) him stuff
6. he feels sick (or) his head and heart hurt
7. they would think badly of him
8. he was with the same kids (or) he found ways to hide his secret

Sequence

9. 4
10. 6
11. 2
12. 3
13. 1
14. 5

Critical Thinking

Answers will vary.

CHAPTER 2

Word Study

1. friend
2. dream
3. toward
4. shower
5. problem
6. cute

Main Idea

Answers may vary along the line of first day at new school.

Inference

- takes his time getting to school
- doesn't want to hurt Dan's feelings
- keeps to himself

Context Clues

1. he's smart
2. he's been hurt or he doesn't want them to know his secret
3. he had friends

Predicting Outcome

Answers will vary.

CHAPTER 3

Word Study

1. different
2. bullies
3. history
4. part
5. short

Details

1. go to school and do homework
2. get the bullies to stop and fill his time

Cause and Effect

1. Tom had tried to get out of answering a question on one of his first days.
2. Mr. Black seemed to know that Tom was different or that he had a secret.

Critical Thinking

Answers will vary.

CHAPTER 4

Main Idea

The main idea in this chapter revolves around the kids debating whether or not they will befriend Tom.

Sequence

1. Beth's face got red
2. Bob left
3. Nick said to give it some time
4. Tom went by
5. Beth left
6. Nick and Dan stopped to talk

Details

1. Beth because he's cute, Dan because he's a good ball player and Kim because she feels sorry for him.
2. Bob and Nick because they think Tom might make trouble.

Character Study

- Dropped his books to get out of answering a question
- He stopped to ask if the little kid he bumped into was okay.

Critical Thinking

Answers will vary.

CHAPTER 5

Details

1. pushed him
2. hit him

Inference

- The kids already knew about the bullies in the school.

Character Study

1. He lets on he doesn't feel anything and he is quiet.
2. He lets on that he doesn't hear the bullies when they yell at him.

Context Clues

He ignores them. He doesn't let them know if they are upsetting him.

Predicting Outcome

Answers will vary.

CHAPTER 6

Word Study

1. mine
2. each
3. great
4. mean
5. week

Main Idea

Answers may vary around "planning to stop the bullies."

Sequence

- 3
- 5
- 1
- 6
- 2
- 4

Cause and Effect

He had seen what the bullies are doing.

Critical Thinking

Answers will vary.

CHAPTER 7

Word Study

1. awesome
2. great/wonderful
3. split/different
4. a short length of time

Cause and Effect

1. things were getting better for him
2. they helped him laugh at himself

Detail

He changed the subject or asked how they were going to raise money.

Context Clues

Beth asked if she could fill in as his girlfriend. He was worried about not having a girlfriend for the fund raiser.

Predicting Outcome

Answers will vary.

CHAPTER 8

***ALL ANSWERS IN CHAPTER 8 WILL VARY.**

My Secret

Skills List

	Chapter 1	Chapter 2	Chapter 3	Chapter 4	Chapter 5	Chapter 6	Chapter 7	Chapter 8
Word Study		✓	✓			✓	✓	
Character	✓			✓	✓			✓
Main Idea		✓		✓		✓		✓
Inference	✓	✓			✓			✓
Sequence	✓			✓		✓		
Cause/ Effect	✓		✓			✓	✓	
Detail			✓	✓	✓		✓	
Context Clues		✓	✓		✓		✓	
Predicting Outcomes		✓			✓		✓	
Critical Thinking	✓			✓		✓		

My Secret

Skills List

Student's Name _____

	Chapter 1	Chapter 2	Chapter 3	Chapter 4	Chapter 5	Chapter 6	Chapter 7	Chapter 8
Word Study								
Character								
Main Idea								
Inference								
Sequence								
Cause/ Effect								
Detail								
Context Clues								
Predicting Outcomes								
Critical Thinking								

My Secret

List of New Vocabulary by Chapter

Chapter 1	Chapter 2	Chapter 3	Chapter 4
<ul><li>answer</li><li>cute</li><li>heart</li><li>late</li><li>moving</li><li>new</li><li>pain</li><li>problem</li><li>science</li><li>sports</li><li>worse</li><li>year</li></ul>	<ul><li>class</li><li>done</li><li>dream</li><li>friend</li><li>hard</li><li>life</li><li>office</li><li>our</li><li>shower</li><li>toward</li></ul>	<ul><li>bullies</li><li>buy</li><li>catch</li><li>different</li><li>every</li><li>gym</li><li>history</li><li>many</li><li>own</li><li>part</li><li>short</li><li>teacher</li></ul>	<ul><li>anything</li><li>bumped</li><li>city</li><li>face</li><li>fact</li><li>fries</li><li>hall</li><li>milk</li><li>question</li><li>seems</li><li>shop</li></ul>
Chapter 5	**Chapter 6**	**Chapter 7**	**Chapter 8**
<ul><li>angry</li><li>anything</li><li>nothing</li><li>read</li></ul>	<ul><li>cool</li><li>coughing</li><li>each</li><li>else</li><li>great</li><li>mean</li><li>mine</li><li>smart</li><li>week</li></ul>	<ul><li>football</li><li>games</li><li>powder puff</li><li>thanks</li></ul>	<ul><li>place</li><li>stand</li></ul>

My Secret

New Vocabulary List

A
- angry
- answer
- anything

B
- bullies
- bumped
- buy

C
- catch
- city
- class
- cool
- coughing
- cute

D
- dream

- different
- done

E
- each
- else
- every

F
- face
- fact
- football
- friend
- fries

G
- games
- great
- gym

H
- hall
- hard
- heart
- history

L
- late
- life

M
- many
- mean
- milk
- mine
- moving

N
- new
- nothing

O
- office
- our
- own

P
- pain
- part
- place
- powder puff
- problem

Q
- question

R
- read

S
- science
- seems
- shop
- short
- shower
- smart
- sports
- stand

T
- teacher
- thanks
- toward

U

V

W
- week
- worse

X

Y
- year

Z